THE BEST DAD JOKES EVER

Patchwork
BOOKS

Copyright © 2023 by Patchwork Books
All rights reserved.

No portion of this book may be reproduced in any form without written permission from the publisher or author, except as permitted by copyright law.

My boss asked why I only get sick on work days.

I said it must be my weekend immune system.

Did you hear about the snail who got rid of his shell?

He thought it would make him faster, but it just made him sluggish.

My wife rearranged the labels on my spice rack.

I haven't confronted her yet but the thyme is cumin.

I used to run a dating service for chickens.

But I struggled to make hens meet.

As I suspected, someone has been adding soil to my garden.

The plot thickens.

I asked the toy store clerk where the Arnold Schwarzenegger action figures were.

She replied "Aisle B, back."

Did you hear about the cheese factory that exploded in France?

There was nothing left but de Brie.

Apparently to start a zoo you need at least two pandas, a grizzly and three polars.

That's the bear minimum.

Sad news, my obese parrot died today.

Mind you, it's a huge weight off my shoulders.

Who decided to call it emotional baggage...

...and not griefcase.

Did you know Marvin Gaye used to keep sheep in his vineyard?

He herded through the grapevine.

I got my daughter a fridge for her birthday.

I can't wait to see her face light up when she opens it.

My friend Jack claims he can communicate with vegetables.

Jack and the beans talk.

In Germany they have a sausage made out of other sausages.

It's the wurst of the wurst.

Lance isn't a common name these days.

But in medieval times, people were named Lance a lot.

I burnt my Hawaiian pizza last night.

I should have put it on aloha setting.

I just found out I'm colorblind.

The news came out of the purple!

I called in a handyman and gave him a list of jobs to do but when I got home only items 1, 3 and 5 had been done.

Turns out he only does odd jobs.

I met a man with a didgeridoo and he was playing Dancing Queen on it.

I thought
'That's Abba-riginal.'

I hate my job—all I do is crush cans all day.

It's soda pressing.

When my wife is sad I let her colour in my tattoos.

She just needs a shoulder to crayon.

I went to the zoo today and saw a slice of toast lying in one of the enclosures.

It was bread in captivity.

Why did the scarecrow win an award?

Because he was out-standing in his field.

Bigfoot is sometimes confused with Sasquatch.

Yeti never complains.

After giving my son two karate lessons, he said he didn't want any more.

Still, at least I got my car washed and my fence painted.

Every time I take my dog to the park, the ducks try to bite him.

That's what I get for buying a pure bread dog.

Karl Marx is a historically famous figure but nobody ever mentions his sister, Onya.

She invented the starting pistol.

My teacher told me I would never be good at poetry because of my dyslexia.

But so far I've made 3 vases and a jug.

"Do you think I reference dinosaurs too much when I write?" I asked.

She was silent, like the p in pterodactyl, but I knew what it meant.

What did Mr. T say to the vegetarian?

I pity tofu.

I got so drunk last night that I started a fight with a mop.

To be fair I wiped the floor with him.

I wondered why the frisbee kept getting bigger and bigger.

Then it hit me.

I was in a job interview yesterday and the interviewer asked if I can perform under pressure?

I said "No, but I know all the words to Bohemian Rhapsody."

Did you hear about the chameleon who couldn't change colour?

He had a reptile dysfunction.

And the lord said unto John "come forth and you shall receive eternal life."

But John came fifth and won a toaster.

"Dad, can you explain solar eclipses?"

No son.

Why do the Norwegians put barcodes on their battleships?

So they can Scandinavian.

I accidentally rubbed ketchup in my eyes.

Now I have Heinzsight.

6:30 is the best time on the clock.

Hands down.

I've started saying mucho to my Mexican friends.

It means a lot to them.

I'm reading a book about anti-gravity.

It's impossible to put down.

I told my wife she drew her eyebrows too high.

She looked surprised.

I had a dream that I was swimming in an ocean of orange soda.

Turns out it was just a Fanta sea.

Where do bad rainbows go?

Prism.

What do you call a magical dog?

A labra-cadabra-dor.

Someone broke into my house and stole my limbo trophy.

How low can you go.

I always knock on the fridge before I open it.

Just in case there's a salad dressing.

Whoever stole my copy of Microsoft Office, you're in big trouble!

You have my Word.

What's Forrest Gump's password?

1forrest1.

I've started telling people about the benefits of dried grapes.

It's all about raisin awareness.

How many paranoid people does it take to change a light bulb?

Who wants to know?

My flat-earther friend decided to walk to the end of the world to prove it is flat.

In the end, he came around.

How does Moses make his tea?

Hebrews it?

100 years ago everyone owned a horse and only the rich had cars.

Now everyone has cars and only the rich have horses.

How the stables have turned.

My wife says I have two faults.

I don't listen...and something else.

My ceiling isn't the best.

But it's up there.

Two windmills are standing in a field and one asks the other "What kind of music do you like?"

The other replies "I'm a big metal fan."

A friend said she doesn't understand cloning.

I said that makes two of us.

RIP boiling water.

You will be mist.

There's only one thing I can't deal with, and that's a deck of cards glued together.

What time did Sean Connery go to Wimbledon?

Tennish.

I told my doctor that I had hearing problems so he asked me to describe the symptoms.

I said Homer's a fat guy and Marge has blue hair.

Bruce Lee was fast but he had an even faster brother.

Sudden Lee.

So many people these days are too judgemental.

I can tell just by looking at them.

What do you call a Frenchman wearing sandals?

Phillipe Phillope.

Why does Snoop Dogg need an umbrella?

Fo drizzle.

Light travels faster than sound.

That's why some people appear bright until you hear them speak.

I'm not a fan of Russian dolls.

They're so full of themselves.

Just bought a boomerang from a ghost.

That'll come back to haunt me.

I never wanted to believe that my dad was stealing from his job as a road worker.

But when I got home, all the signs were there.

A man just assaulted me with milk, cream and butter.

How dairy.

I love jokes about eyes.

The cornea the better.

I tripped over my wife's bra.

It was a boobie trap.

What do you call James Bond taking a bath?

Bubble 07.

My boss calls me 'The computer'.

Nothing to do with intelligence, I just go to sleep if left unattended for 15 minutes.

My mum just found out I replaced her bed with a trampoline

She hit the roof!

You've really got to hand it to short people…

Because they usually can't reach it anyway.

I lost 25% of my roof last night...

oof.

I asked the lion in my wardrobe what he was doing in there.

He said it was Narnia business.

A shark can swim faster than me, but I can run faster than a shark.

So in a triathlon, it would come down to who is the better cyclist.

Dogs can't operate MRI machines.

But cats can.

To the man who invented zero.

Thanks for nothing.

My wife is leaving me due to my obsession with Star Wars.

I told her, "May divorce be with you."

What's the difference between black eye peas and chick peas?

Black eye peas can sing us a song but chick peas can only hummus one.

Shout out to the people asking what the opposite of in is.

I want to tell you about a woman who eats plants.

You've probably never heard of herbivore.

How do you confuse an idiot?

Made in United States
Troutdale, OR
12/19/2023